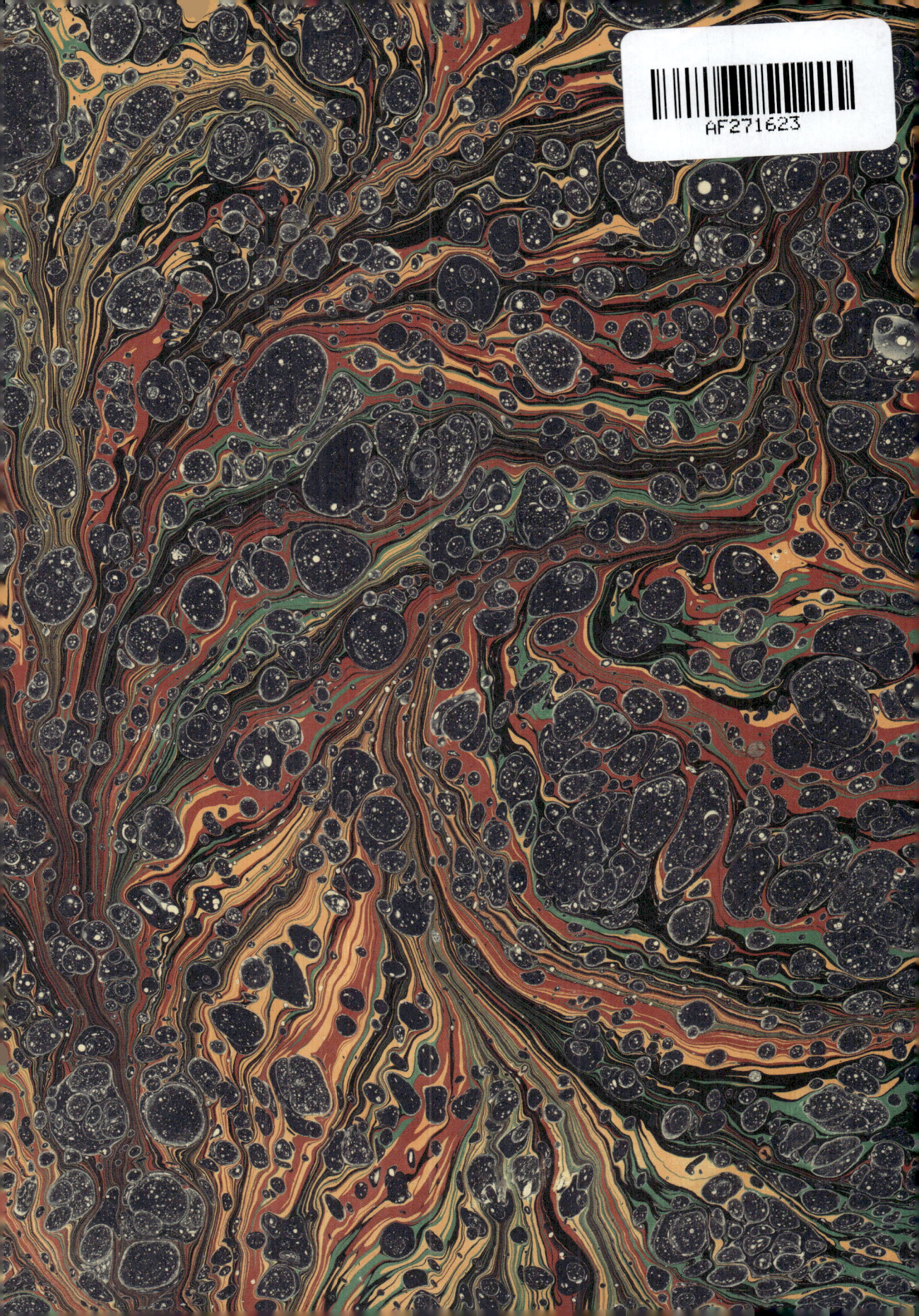

GERMAN WOUND BADGES
IN WORLD WAR II

Rolf Michaelis

Schiffer Military History
Atglen, PA

Translation from the German by Dr. Edward Force.

Book Design by Stephanie Daugherty.

Copyright © 2012 by Schiffer Publishing.
Library of Congress Control Number: 2012942403

Printed in China.
ISBN: 978-0-7643-4259-2

This book was originally published in German under the title
Die deutschen Verwundetenabzeichen by Michaelis-Verlag.

We are interested in hearing from authors with book ideas on related topics.

Published by Schiffer Publishing Ltd.
4880 Lower Valley Road
Atglen, PA 19310
Phone: (610) 593-1777
FAX: (610) 593-2002
E-mail: Info@schifferbooks.com.
Visit our web site at: www.schifferbooks.com
Please write for a free catalog.
This book may be purchased from the publisher.
Try your bookstore first.

In Europe, Schiffer books are distributed by:
Bushwood Books
6 Marksbury Avenue
Kew Gardens
Surrey TW9 4JF, England
Phone: 44 (0) 20 8392-8585
FAX: 44 (0) 20 8392-9876
E-mail: Info@bushwoodbooks.co.uk.
Visit our website at: www.bushwoodbooks.co.uk

CONTENTS

Foreword

The subject of wounds has scarcely been mentioned in post-war German literature. This is surprising, as millions of soldiers and civilians sacrificed their physical and psychological health in the wars.

The book before you, now issued in its fourth edition, shall fill this gap. Along with the object, the Wound Badge itself, the related topic of transporting and treating wounded men will be taken up. The treatment will also show what immediate misery war brings with it.

Rolf Michaelis
Berlin, June 2007

THE WORLD WAR I WOUND BADGE

On March 3, 1918, Kaiser Wilhelm II created a medal such as had never yet existed in this form in Germany: the medal for the wounded. In the documentation, the German Emperor and King of Prussia expressed the reason behind it:

> I wish to award this badge as a special recognition for the Fatherland's wounded. This badge shall recognize those who bled for the Fatherland or lost their health to enemy action in the war zone and thus became incapable of service.

The idea of creating a medal for the wounded resulted from the fact that the number of wounds, especially serious ones, had exceeded everything previously known to an unimaginable extent in the bloody battles of attrition and position of World War I. While in previous wars, which did not have the extent and mass of World War I, a wound was considered equal to bravery as a rule, so that a medal for bravery could be awarded, the situation changed with the thousands of soldiers who were wounded in their positions by endless artillery fire without actual contact with enemy troops. In 1917 the idea was born to create a special badge for these wounded men.

The awarding of the badge was limited at first to the Prussian states. But on March 11, 1918 it was extended to the Kingdom of Bavaria, which had had a special position within the German Reich since 1866. After the Medal of Honor could be awarded only to the Army and the air units subordinated to the Army, a wound badge for the Navy was introduced on June 24, 1918. As of July 8, 1918, the badge also applied to colonial troops.

In all, there were three stages of the badge, which was worn on the left chest side:

> The black Wound Badge for first and second wounds.

> The matte white Wound Badge for third and fourth wounds.

> The matte yellow Wound Badge for fifth and subsequent wounds.

The badges in black were pressed hollow in sheet iron, the white and yellow badges were made hollow in sheet brass and showed a 1916 model German steel helmet on a grainy background for the Army, lying on two antique swords and framed by a laurel wreath. The badge for the Navy showed an anchor lying on two antique swords on a grainy background and encircled by an anchor chain. On the back of each was a pin for attaching the badge to a uniform.

On civilian clothing the badge could also be worn as a miniature – on a miniature chain, as a miniature pin or a buttonhole decoration. Many soldiers, especially officers, were happy to obtain versions of the badge offered by craftsmen and jewelers back home. There were many variations: for example, the Wound Badge made of 800 silver, or on one or more screwplates, or a pierced variant without the grainy background – which was not officially authorized.

During the demobilization in 1919-1920 the unit dispersal staffs still awarded badges to mustered-out soldiers.

As of January 30, 1936, on the third anniversary of Hitler's seizure of power in 1933, German soldiers, plus foreigners serving in German units, in World War I who did not yet have a Wound Badge could apply for it from the appropriate supply offices. They had to provide proof of their wounding in the form of a militarily attested document. The supply offices that were responsible for keeping order or supplying the applicable former soldiers ware also authorized. Germans who were located outside the country could also send in the application, and it was sent on appropriately.

In the supply offices, 442,669 badges were requested by the time the application period ended (December 31, 1936). Of them, 46,700 applications were turned down – 28,000 applications could not be processed by July 1, 1937, so that a later dating of the documents is quite possible.

By July 1, 1937, some 290,000 applications for the black badge, 71,000 for the white and 7,000 for the yellow badge were awarded.

By the authorization of January 30, 1936 former war participants could receive the white badge regardless of the number of their wounds if the wound had resulted in the loss of a hand, foot, eye, loss of hearing in both ears, serious brain damage or unsightly facial wounds that made associating with people difficult.

The matte yellow badge could be obtained by one who had suffered several aforementioned wounds or had been blinded and received care.

After their inclusion in the German Reich, Austria, the Sudetenland and Memelland were also included in awarding the badge.

Wounded German soldiers in Alsace.

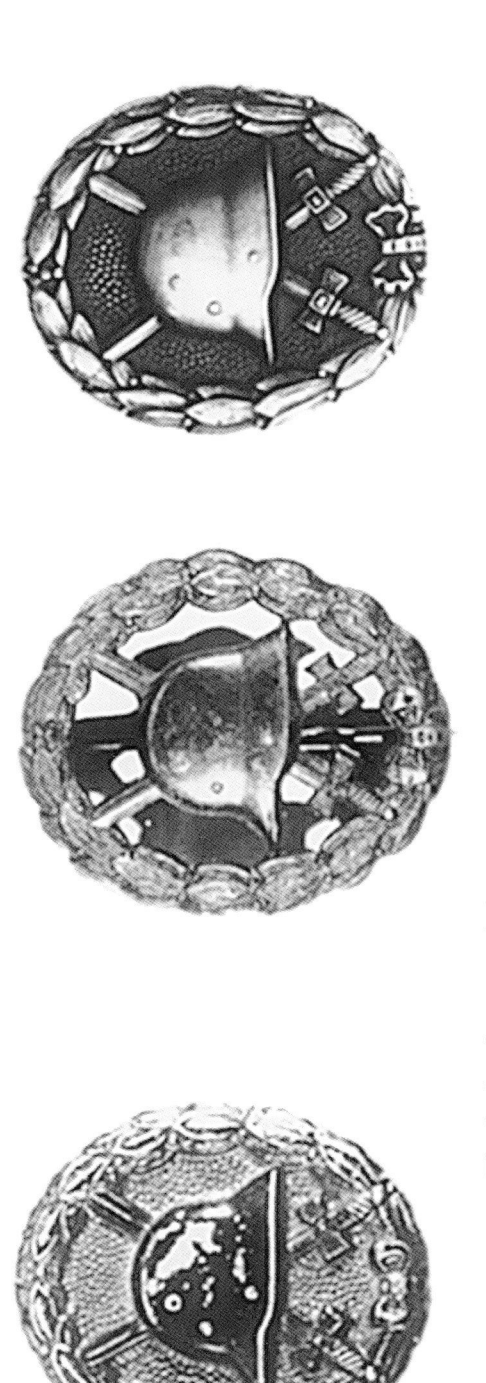

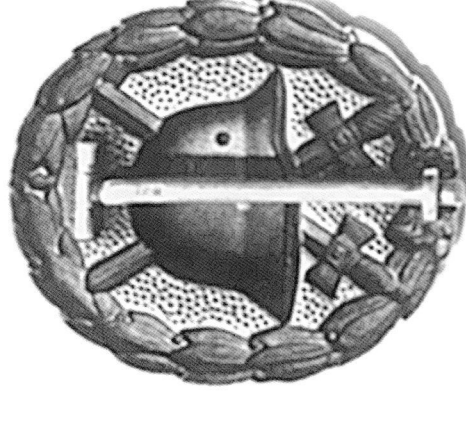

The badge for wounded Army soldiers as of 1918 (front and rear sides).

Pierced version.

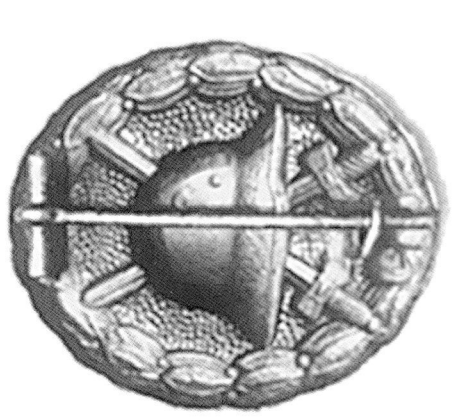

Official version.

8

The badge for wounded Navy sailors as of 1918.

The badge container.

**This soldier wears both the ribbon for the Iron Cross II
and the black Wound Badge.**

The NCO at right received the Iron Cross II plus the silver Wound Badge.

Miniature chains with the badge for the Navy (above) and Army (below).

Buttonhole decoration (enlarged).

12

Beſitzzeugnis
über das
Verwundeten-Abzeichen

Dem ___*Hauptm Behr,*___
___*Stab Art. Kdeur. 85*___
ist das Abzeichen für ___1___ malige Verwundung
gemäß A.V. Bl. 1918 G 169/170 ___ verliehen worden.
___Grodno___, den ___24. 4. 1918___

Krohn
Generalmajor.

ZEICHNUNG VON UFFZ FRED HENDRIOK   DRUCK. ZEITUNG DER 10. ARMEE.

The decorative certificate for the Wound Badge in black from World War I.

The Legion Condor's Wound Badge

The service of German volunteers in the Legion Condor during the Spanish Civil War led Hitler to award the Wound Badge, on May 22, 1939, in its black and – for the first time, in place of the matte white–silver forms:

> "As an honoring symbol of remembrance for those German volunteers who were wounded or damaged by enemy weapons while putting down Bolshevism in the Spanish war of liberation as members of the Legion Condor or in connection with their service and combat action with the German Navy in Spanish waters."

In production and material, it was like that of the Army in 1918, differing only in having a swastika on the helmet. The awarding requirements were the same as in 1918 and the extension of 1936, though no golden or matte yellow badge was included. This version of the badge was awarded to the wounded men via the troops until early in the Russian campaign. There were variations in the form of a pierced and a hollowed type, in which a base was soldered to the hollowed emblem.

The World War II Wound Badge

On September 1, 1939, the day of the German attack on Poland, Hitler repeated the awarding of the Wound Badge. It could be awarded, *"as an honor for those who, in the brave action of their person for the Fatherland, have been wounded or damaged by the effect of enemy weapons"* to wounded:

– Germans

– Ethnic Germans who had shown their German ethnicity, sworn an oath to Hitler, and served in the German Wehrmacht

– Foreign volunteers who swore an oath to Hitler and fought within or in units of the German Army and Waffen-SS

– Volunteers of foreign peoples in regions "liberated" from Bolshevism.

It looked similar to the Wound Badge of the Legion Condor but bore, instead of the M-16 steel helmet, the smaller Model M-235 helmet.

The badges in black were stamped in sheet brass at the beginning of the war, and later of sheet iron, while the silver and gold badges were at first made of brass as well, and later of fine zinc. The manufacturers also stamped in their trademark in the form of a number code.

The Wound Badge could be awarded, as there was no copyright on it. Awarding to undeserving persons could be ruled out by those in charge of awarding it. Particular value was placed on the formulation of *"brave action of the person"*. This was always seen as essential where no obvious objection to awarding was found – such as "cowardly behavior". The principle was:

"The sign of honor must be gained in honor."

Helmut Uphoff remembers his wound:

I was wounded on July 6, 1941 on the Keskimes before Salla on the German-Finnish front. In attack on the fortifications near Salla I took a machine-gun burst of five explosive shots in the legs and bled unbelievably. I was carried by comrades to our main dressing station (HVP) and received my first treatment there. On the next day I was taken on a stretcher through the wooded country to Field Hospital (mot.) 617. By ambulance I reached War Hospital 1/521 on July 8. I was very lucky that nobody thought of radical measures (amputation). A few days later I was taken to Kemi on a hospital train and then on to Tornio. After going a few meters on foot I was taken on Hospital Train 661 through Sweden via Lulea, Umsa, Sundsvall, Upsala, Stockholm, Orebro and Karlstadt to Oslo. There I got on the hospital ship "Stuttgart" and reached Kiel at the end of July 1941. On July 31 I arrived in Bad Harzburg by hospital train and was housed at the reserve hospital in the "Harzburger Hof" hotel. After my wound healed, I was released to the reserve troops already at the end of August. Since this unit (SS Replacement Battalion "A" in Goslar) was no longer responsible for me, I was transferred to the SS Replacement Battalion "Nord" in Wehlau. At first I went to the recovery company, in which there were soldiers who had come directly out of hospitals. In September I was then transferred to the 3rd Company and given recovery leave. On the way back from leave the wound became inflamed and I was sent on September 28, 1941 to the Reserve Hospital in Posen (Section II, *Wiesenstrasse*). On October 15 I returned to the SS Replacement Battalion "Nord", which I volunteered to leave after a few days."

The awarding could also be neglected in those cases in which the awarding contradicted the meaning of the honor. The superiors who made the decision could decide that minor wounds were not to be included. As for accidents in training, caused by malfunctioning weapons or ammunition, in the testing of weapons or simple illness, the requirements were not fulfilled, even if they took place right at the front.

Wounds by enemy weapon effect, to be sure, were considered equal to such wounds or damage that had taken place in connection with a combat action, caused by one's own weapons, without one being personally to blame.

Several wounds that took place at the same time counted as one. Wounds were counted as happening at the same time if they were caused by the same weapon at the same moment (for example, a machine-gun burst or several fragments from a grenade). Earlier wounds, for which a Wound Badge had already been given, were counted toward the awarding of the next higher step. This regulation also applied to wounds suffered in World War I or the Spanish Civil War. Only the most recently awarded class could be worn; the badge from World War I or the Spanish Civil War had to be removed for a new awarding.

Taking up or defusing German or enemy mines or duds and laying German or enemy mines against the enemy, as well as the oversight of minefields, were to be regarded as equal to combat action. The Wound Badge could be awarded to soldiers who were wounded or damaged in these jobs not by their own fault. The same applied to wounds that were caused by blockading action (explosions, etc.) within the combat zone, when the commanded securing measures had to be disregarded because of the battle situation.

For the duration of the combat on the eastern front (for Serbia in the winter of 1941-1942), the conditions for awarding could also be regarded as fulfilled if, in cases of freezing in connection with combat action, serious and lasting damage to the body – mainly amputations – occurred. Other than that, sicknesses with resulting lasting damages to the body (such as kidney damage) did not fulfill the awarding conditions.

The concept of "combat actions" should not be confused with "action under enemy fire". All the action in supply service, transport to and from the front, action in the surveillance, security and work services likewise applied in connection with combat action. The effect of enemy weapons could also result from air raids, assassinations, sabotage, paratroop action, etc. The borderline point here was that the weapon effect had to come from an enemy not limited in his freedom of action. Wounds from escaped prisoners of war generally were not counted as wounds if actual combat was not involved. Injuries in train wrecks or accidents in public transport had to result from an enemy attack with direct use of weapons against the train, etc. (for example, hitting a mine, attaching explosives to a train, air attack on the train itself, etc.) For other war-resulting accidents, even if they could be traced directly back to sabotage, and accidents caused by the disabling or damage of transit facilities (signals, rails), the Wound Badge was not to be awarded.

The awarding of the Wound Badge to Wehrmacht members and non-members (such as Waffen-SS, RAD or NSKK) who were subordinated to the Wehrmacht was done by their superior officers from battalion commanders upward, or if necessary by the chief doctor of the responsible medical service office at which the wounded man was treated, by reporting to the troop unit.

For soldiers under punishment, a strict determination was to be applied in testing the circumstances as concerned their misdeeds. Those who had the authority had in all cases to get the facts from the disciplinary officers before the awarding.

The awarding of the badge to members of the units subordinated to the *Reichsführer-SS*, as long as they were not subordinated to the Wehrmacht or fought along with the Wehrmacht, and for members of units subordinated to the chief of the partisan-fighting units, was to be done directly by the *Reichsführer-SS*.

Non-members of the Wehrmacht not listed among the preceding groups could be awarded the badge retroactively to September 1, 1939 by the territorial commanders of the Wehrmacht if they had been wounded by enemy weapons in the occupied areas, the General Government, the Protectorate of Bohemia and Moravia or the homeland war zone.

One exception here concerned those wounded in connection with enemy air attacks. In order to regard the behavior of the entire population as brave under enemy air attacks, the Wound Badge could be awarded retroactively as of September 1, 1939 to all German civilians who were wounded or damaged by enemy action during air raids. The awarding was done by the air district command.

To those soldiers who had to be discharged from military service because of their wound or damage, the leaders of the Army discharge offices could be awarded the badge on their discharge, as could already discharged soldiers by the war zone commanders. Posthumous awarding, though, was not allowed.

For the German soldiers there were five institutions that could award the Wound Badge:

- the Front troop unit

- the replacement troop unit

- the field or reserve hospital

- the military discharge office, when the soldier had to be discharged because of his wounds

- the defense zone command, when the soldier had already been discharged.

The awarding of the badge to the soldier was to be done in worthy form by a superior officer. Direct sending of the badge to the wounded man by the field troop unit was not allowed. The medals were given in award bags, cases or boxes.

The awarding of a badge of honor, like other badges, first had to be approved. The allowed awarding of decorations and badges of honor normally had to be documented by appropriate lists of awardings by the commanders of the units under their command, who had the authority to award them. Only for the wound medal were no lists of recipients required! The empowered commanders simply filled out possession documents. The day of the award was to be entered in the recipient's personal papers, especially his *soldbuch*.

The hospitals of the field and replacement armies reported every award of a Wound Badge on Form 6 b of the H.Dv.21 IInd Part to the replacement troop unit responsible for the recipient. If the recipient still belonged to the field army, the report was also to be sent to the field troop unit.

Wounds could be divided into three categories:

- slight wounds, such as slight splinter wounds or simple grazing shots, which allowed remaining with the front unit or in its medical facilities,

- medium wounds, after the treatment of which in a hospital the soldier was again ready for service,

- serious wounds, which no longer allowed further front service.

A former soldier recalls his slight wound:

"In an enemy grenade-launcher attack, my unit was in a patch of woods. There were numerous "tree-killers", grenades that exploded in the crowns of trees. The effect was even greater. We immediately sought shelter and made ourselves as small targets as possible. Suddenly I felt a stab in my privates, was perplexed at first, and then cried aloud, 'I am hit! Help!' A comrade came quickly and said to me, 'Calm down, you only got a splinter in your behind.' I calmed down and had no particular pains. The shock was greater than the wound – our troop doctor removed the small splinter, swabbed me with iodine, stuck a bandage on and released me with the remark, 'March off.'"

The Wound Badge in black was to be awarded for first and second wounds. For single wounds of unusual types – severe abdominal and chest shots, genital wounds, cripplings and stiffenings of limbs and borderline cases in which limbs etc. were no longer fully unusable – at first only the black medal was awarded. Only after the lasting results of the wound were finally clear could an application for awarding of the higher level of the wound badge be made to the OKH/PA/P5 through channels for consideration.

The Wound Badge in silver was awarded as a rule for third and fourth wounds or damages. Before the badge for several wounds was awarded, the number of wounds was to be determined without objection. The badge could be awarded without reference to the number of wounds if the third damage level was reached. This meant:

– the loss of an arm or leg

– the loss of both feet

– the loss of both lower legs with functioning knee joints remaining

– practical blinding of both eyes (counting number of fingers as a distance of two meters no longer possible), half-side blindness with the loss of the middle retinas or the lower halves of the field of vision,

–disfigurement of the face,

– full stiffening of the spinal column,

– brain or spinal cord wounds with severe functional disturbance.

The golden Wound Badge was awarded from the fifth wound on, or when the fourth damage level was reached. This meant:

– the loss of both hands or legs

– the loss of a hand or foot on three or more limbs

– the loss of a leg and a hand

– the loss or full blinding of both eyes (counting fingers not possible)

– brain or spinal cord wounds with most serious functional disturbance

The first awarding of a golden Wound Badge took place during the Polish campaign, to an officer who already held the World War I Wound Badge.

War-blinded or more severely wounded men of damage levels III and IV could also be promoted to one rank above plan, if their self-control and overall behavior did not rule out the promotion. Their permanent service unfitness and damage, though, had to be determined by the judgment of military doctors. In all cases the promotion of the wounded had to be announced by the troop unit to which the wounded soldier had belonged when wounded. If the troop unit was disbanded, then the checking and decision as to whether the promotion could be announced was done by the representative (homeland) general command. Promotion after the service time of soldiers who were wounded or sick in hospitals was to be announced by the replacement troop unit to which the soldier was transferred during his hospital stay, as long as the troop unit had no objection. A sick man in a hospital was regarded as transferred to a replacement troop unit:

– with their admission to a reserve hospital.

– after four weeks of hospital treatment, if the hospital patient had been admitted to a hospital of the field army or the field troop unit of the patient in the homeland war zone, or the admitting hospital was in the area of operation.

The promotion was announced by the leader of the Army discharge office when the replacement troop unit had neglected to announce the promotion approved by the field unit, or the soldier had already been assigned to the Army discharge office or had already been discharged by it before the service book arrived with the authorization of the field troop unit.

The unplanned promotion could be undertaken on the basis of H.Dv. 29 a Section 37 Item 4, which states:

> "Promotion to *Gefreite*, *Obergefreite*, *Stabsgefreite*, *Unteroffizier*, *Unterfeldwebel* and *Stabsfeldwebel* may be announced at any time. Beyond that, war-blinded and most severely damaged men of damage level III may be promoted one rank over plan as long as functioning and overall condition do not rule out the promotion. Their permanent unfitness for service and damage must be determined by military doctors' judgment."

In addition, such seriously wounded men could also be awarded the Iron Cross II. Class if they did not hold it already.

During World War II, of the estimated sixteen million German soldiers (including Volkssturm, RAD, Hitler Youth, etc.), some six million were wounded. The highest percentage belonged to the Army and the Waffen-SS, followed by the Luftwaffe and finally the Navy. How many Wound Badges of the three levels were awarded cannot be determined for lack of documentation, but, for example, remaining statistics of the 6th SS Mountain Division "Nord" show that in the course of 1942:

1,056 Wound Badges in Black,

68 Wound Badges in Silver, and

1 Wound Badge in Gold

were awarded.

In all, some three million black, 1.5 million silver and 750,000 gold badges may have been awarded,

The Wound Badge of July 20, 1944

After Count Schenk von Stauffenberg's attempt to assassinate Hitler on July 20, 1944, Hitler awarded all soldiers who were wounded in the attack a special Wound Badge in three levels. For the first time, a medal could also be awarded posthumously.

The badges were all made of solid silver – the first stage painted black, the third gilded – and were very similar to the normal Wound Badge. To be sure, the helmet was somewhat smaller and moved upward; under it was the date, 20 July 1944, with Hitler's autograph.

Wound Badges of the Legion Condor (front and back).

Above: official issue; below: hollowed version.

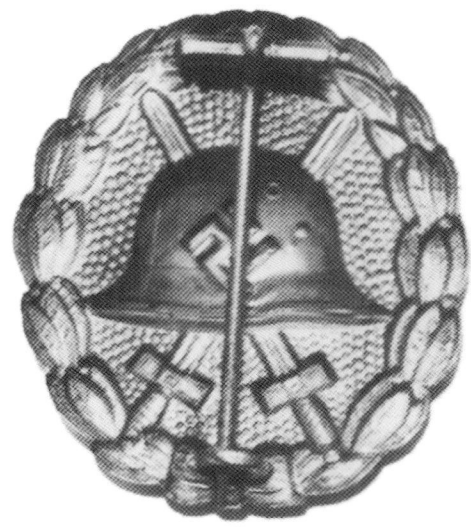

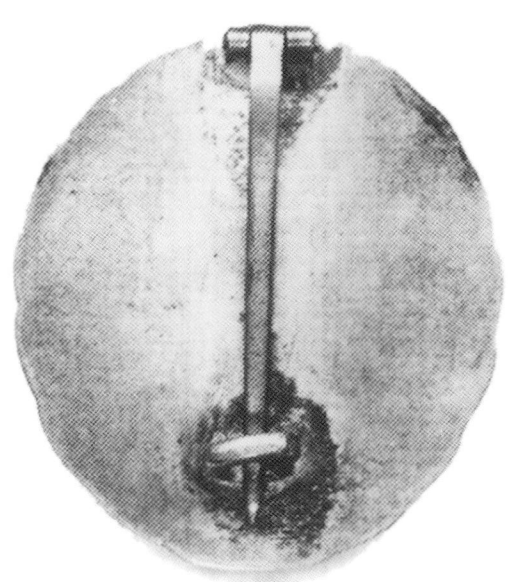

This *Obergefreite* wears the Legion Condor version of the Wound Badge.

A Wound Badge in black in the so-called pierced form of the Legion Condor version.

Kurt Rodde wears the Legion Condor version of the Wound Badge in Silver under the honor pin of the SS-Heimwehr Danzig.

The Wound Badge in Black in the rare award case of the LDO.

The Wound Badge in Black was made by hollow pressing.

Wound Badges in Silver in a fairly uncommon half-full version.
The manufacturer's trademark is also added once again in a recessed area.

Front and back of the
Wound Badge in Gold,
made in massive form.

Soldbuch of a soldier who was awarded, among others, the Wound Badge in Gold.

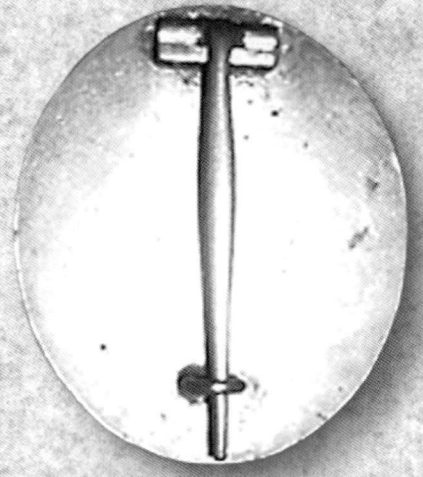

For those wounded in the attempt to assassinate Hitler
on July 20, 1944, a special Wound Badge
of 800-grade silver was made in massive form.

Manufacturer "L/21" in the grainy background on the back.

Manufacturer "L/21" under the pin hook, with a silver indication.

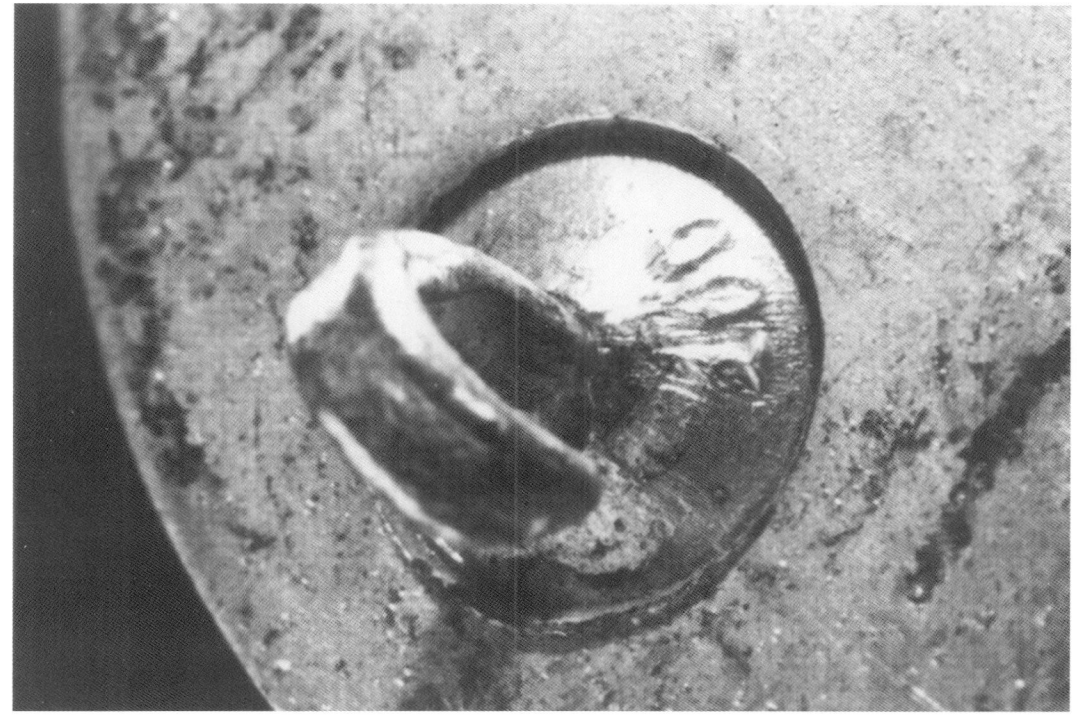

Manufacturer's "100" mark on the pin hook.

Manufacturer's "26" mark on the pin.

Manufacturer "L/11" on the steel helmet on the back.

Manufacturer "L/14" in the steel helmet on the back.

Miniature pins on 8 and 16mm sizes.

The way the Wound Badge was worn on the left chest side.

Members of the police with Wound Badges.

A war-blinded soldier with the Wound Badge in Gold.

Div.Nachschubführer (mot) 160 O.U., den 29.6.42

Betr.: Verleihung eines Verwundetenabzeichens.
Bezug: Dort.Schreiben vom 16.Juni 1942

Herrn
Div.Intendanten
60. Inf. Div. (mot).

> 60. Inf.-Div. (mot.)
> Akt.: IV U
> am 30. JUNI 1942 Anl.
> Nr. 1

Intendant 60. Div.
eingeg.: 30.6.42
Unt.:

    In der Anlage wird Verwundetenabzeichen in schwarz mit
Besitzzeugnis für den am 5.6.42 durch feindl. Fliegerangriff ver-
wundeten Gefreiten Erich Wensurski überreicht.

This *Gefreite* was wounded while a member of a bakery company during an enemy air raid.

Besitzzeugnis

Dem

Erich Wensurski, Gefreiter
[Name, Dienstgrad]

Bäckerei-Kompanie (mot) 160
[Truppenteil, Dienststelle]

ist auf Grund

seiner am ...5. Juni 1942... erlittenen

...1. maligen Verwundung oder Beschädigung

das

Verwundetenabzeichen

in ...schwarz...

verliehen worden.

...Russland..., den 19.Juni 19 42

[Unterschrift]

Major u. Kommandeur

[Dienstgrad und Dienststelle]

Besitzeugnis

Dem

Hans-Eberhard Kratz, Uffz.,

(Name, Dienstgrad)

1./Gren.Rgt.105

(Truppenteil, Dienststelle)

ist auf Grund seiner am 15.7.44 um 7.00, 11.00
und 14.00 Uhr,

erlittenen 3 maligen Verwundung ~~oder Beschädigung~~ das

Verwundetenabzeichen

in SILBER verliehen worden

Im Felde, den 10. August 1944

(Ort, Datum)

Im Auftrage: I. Bataillon
Grenadier - Regiment 105

J.V. H a u p t m a n n .
(Unterschrift, Dienstgrad und Dienststelle)

Bestell-Nr. 608. Wkr.-Dr. XII Wiesbaden

This *Unteroffizier* was wounded three times in one day!

BESITZZEUGNIS

DEM

Leutnant Anton M e i s t e r

(NAME, DIENSTGRAD)

2./Fest.M.G.Batl.5o

(TRUPPENTEIL, DIENSTSTELLE)

IST AUF GRUND

SEINER AM ___18. 11. 1944___ ERLITTENEN

5 MALIGEN VERWUNDUNG – ~~BESCHÄDIGUNG~~

DAS

VERWUNDETENABZEICHEN

IN ___G o l d___

VERLIEHEN WORDEN.

Badgastein ___, DEN 4. 1. 19 45___

(UNTERSCHRIFT)

Oberstarzt u.Chefarzt d.Res.Laz.III

(DIENSTGRAD UND DIENSTSTELLE)

After the fifth wound, this *Leutnant* was awarded the Wound Badge in Gold.

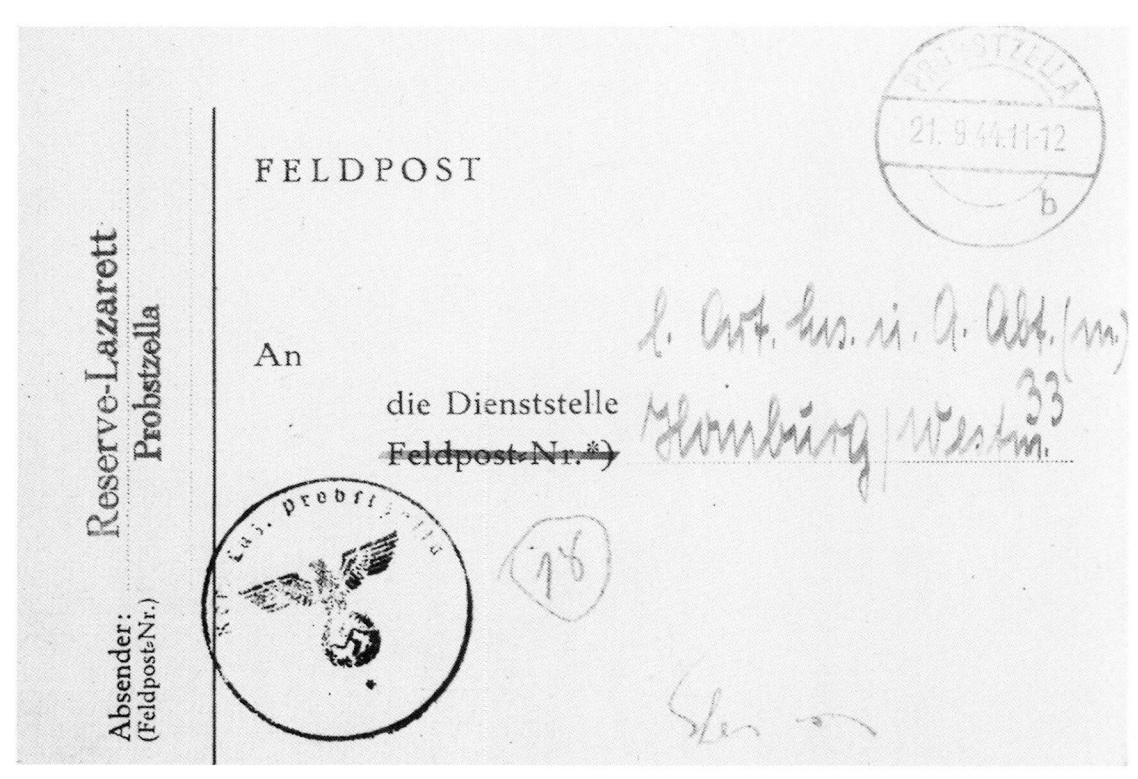

Report of a hospital to a replacement unit on the admission of a wounded soldier.

Reserve-Lazarett

Probstzella

....
(Bezeichnung der Sanitätseinheit und Feldpost-Nr.)

Formblatt 6, I zu K.S.V. (H), Teil II, Nr. 16a
Anlage 1 zu A.H.M. 1944, § 123

........................, den 16. 9. 194 4
(Ort und Datum)

des ....
(Dienstgrad)

Meldung über Lazarett-Aufnahme

.... 12. 5. 20. .... 57 502 6
(Vor- und Familienname)   (Geburtsdatum)   (Geburtsort)   (Feldpost-Nr. seines Truppenteils)

Nur ausfüllen bei Offz., die als zum Ers.-Truppenteil versetzt gelten! a) Letzter Feld-Truppenteil b) Zuständiger Ers.-Truppenteil c) Zuständiges WMA. oder WBK. (Soldbuch S. 4) d) Wehrnummer (Soldbuch S. 1)	a) Erkennungsmarke b) Genaue Anschrift Letzter Friedens-Truppenteil a) Rangdienstalter, Ord.-Nr. u. Angabe, ob aktiv, d. R. oder z. V. c) Zuständiger Wehrkreis d) Letzte Verwendung und seit wann? und bei SS-Führern im Offizierrang Staatsangehörigkeit	a) Krankheitsbezeichnung (Art der Verwundung oder Erkrankung) b) Voraussichtlicher Tauglichkeits-grad nach Abschluß der Lazarett-behandlung u. Behandlungsdauer	a) In das hiesige Lazarett aufgenommen am? b) Seit wann in Lazarett-behandlung (Tag der 1. Lazarettaufnahme, siehe Soldbuch S. 12/13
a)	a)	a)	a) 16. 9. 44.
b)	b)	b) ca. 6 - 8 Wochen	b) 16. 9. 44.
c)	c)		
d)	d)		

Sind die Angehörigen benachrichtigt? ....

1. Falls der Erkrankte oder Verstorbene im Truppenkrankenbuch noch nicht eingetragen ist, hat die Eintragung zu erfolgen. Die Ersatztruppenteile tragen jedoch Angehörige des Feldheeres, die in Reservelazarette verlegt worden sind, nicht in das Truppenkrankenbuch ein. Dagegen hat jeder Ersatztruppenteil die Pflicht, sofort nach
Eingang eines Formbl. 6, I die Karteimittel (Wehrpaß mit Strafbuchauszug, Wehrstammbuch und Gesundheitsbuch) beizuziehen.
2. Dem Truppenarzt ist diese Meldung nach Eingang und Kenntnisnahme sofort vorzulegen. Der Erkrankungs- oder Todesfall ist im nächstfälligen Truppenkrankennachweis
zu berücksichtigen, wenn die Fall erst auf Grund dieser Meldung in das Truppenkrankenbuch eingetragen wurde. In Lazaretten Verstorbene sind auf die 1. Seite des Truppen-
krankennachweises in den Spalten "fort." in Abgang zu bringen.

.... **Stabsarzt**
(Unterschrift, Dienstgrad)

Zu beziehen vom Streitberger-Verlag, Pößneck
Bestellnr. W. 501a

35 744 W. 1810

41

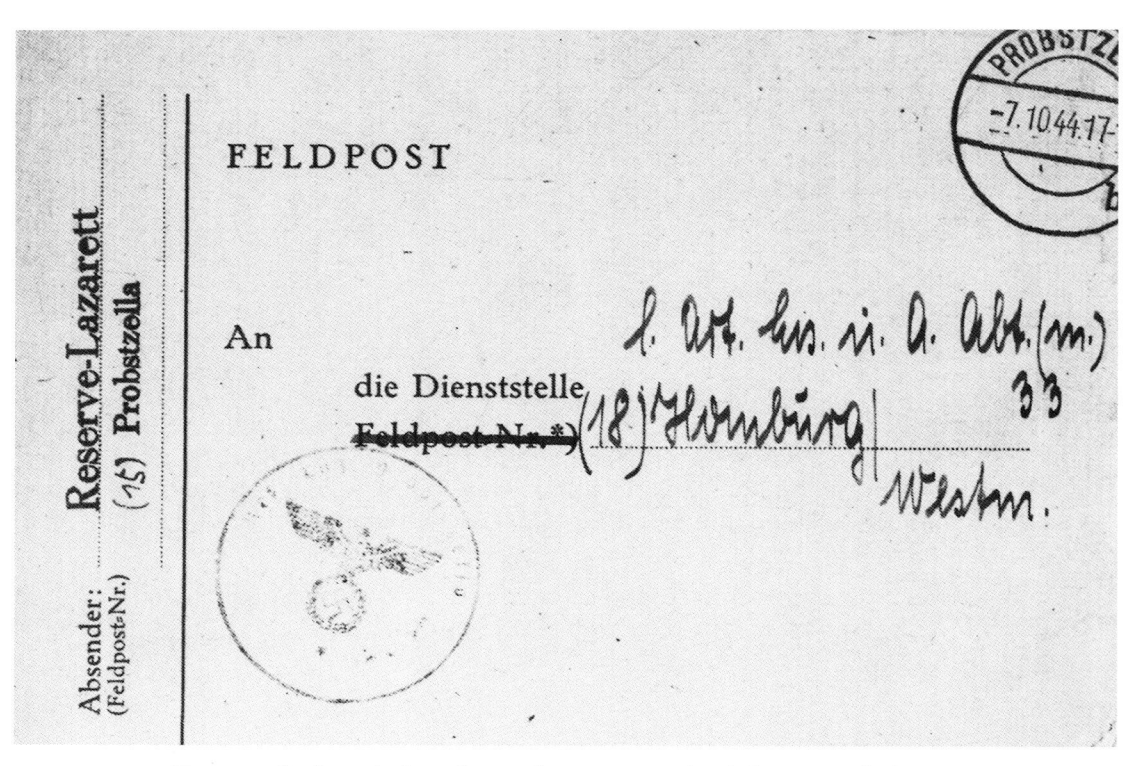

**Report of a hospital to the replacement unit of the wounded man
on his transfer to another hospital.**

Formblatt 6, II zu K.S.V. (H), Teil II, Nr. 16a
Anlage 2 zu A.H.M. 1944, § 123

Reserve-Lazarett
Probstzella

(Bezeichnung der Sanitätseinheit und Feldpostnr.)

................................., den 6. 10. 194. 4.
(Ort und Datum)

Meldung über Lazarett=Abgang (Verlegung, Entlassung zur Truppe und Todesfälle)

des ....
(Dienstgrad)   (Vor- und Familienname)   (Geburtsdatum)   (Geburtsort)   (Feldpost=Nr. seines Truppenteils)

			Urlaub wurde erteilt
	a) Erkennungsmarke b) Genaue Heimatanschrift	a) Krankheitsbezeichnung (Art der Verwundung oder Erkrankung) b) Seit wann in Lazarettbehandlung? (Tag der 1. Lazarettaufnahme, siehe Soldbuch S. 12/13)	Abgang a) am? (Datum) b) Abgangsart, z.B. „gestorben", mit „L.Z. 1134 in rückwärt. Laz. verlegt", „ins Res.-Laz. 103 Berlin verlegt", „dfg. zur Truppe, kv. nach 3 Wochen Urlaub"	a) Urlaubart b) von .... bis .... c) wohin? (nur ausfül- len, wenn Urlauber nicht zum Lazarett, sondern zur Truppe zurückzukehren hat)
a) Letzter Feld=Truppenteil b) Zuständiger Ersatz=Truppenteil				
1	2	3	4	5

Sind die Angehörigen benachrichtigt? ....
(ja oder nein)

1. Falls der Erkrankte oder Verstorbene im Truppenkrankenbuch noch nicht eingetragen ist, hat die Eintragung zu erfolgen. Die Ersatztruppenteile tragen jedoch Angehörige des Feldheeres, die in Reservelazarette verlegt worden sind, nicht in ihr Truppenkrankenbuch ein. Dagegen hat jeder Ersatztruppenteil die Pflicht, sofort nach Eingang eines Formbl. 6, I die Karteimittel (Wehrpaß mit Strafbuchauszug, Wehrstammbuch und Gesundheitsbuch) beizuziehen.

2. Dem Truppenarzt ist diese Meldung nach Eingang mit dem Truppenkrankenbuch vorzulegen. Der Erkrankungs- oder Todesfall ist im nächstfälligen Truppenkrankennachweis zu berücksichtigen, wenn der Fall erst auf Grund dieser Meldung in das Truppenkrankenbuch eingetragen wurde. Lazaretten Verstorbene sind auf der 1. Seite des Truppen- krankennachweises in den Spalten „ins Lazarett", ... „Abgang durch Tod" in Abgang zu bringen.

....
(Unterschrift, Dienstgrad)

Zu beziehen vom Streitberger=Verlag, Pößneck
Bestellnr. W. 501 b

25 444 W.

Feldpost

SAALFELD (SAALE) 1
28.10.44. -10

Der

Dienststelle

Feldpostnummer: 5 7 50 2 C

Report of a hospital to the troop unit on the accomplished
awarding of the Wound Badge in Black.

Reserve-Lazarett S aalfeld/Saale.   Saalfeld, den   27.1o.1944
Az.: .... 29...

Betr.: Verleihung des Verwundetenabzeichens.

Der
Dienststelle
Fp.Nr. 57 5o2 C ....

Dem...Obgefr.Josef.S.p.r.a.n.g.e.r..., der zuletzt der dortigen
Einheit angehörte, ist heute auf Grund seiner am..12..9..1944...
erlittenen..einmaligen...Verwundung das Verwundetenabzeichen
in...schwarz....verliehen worden. Um Eintragung in die Karteimittel wird gebeten.

~~Sollte das Verwundetenabzeichen zu Unrecht verliehen worden~~
~~sein, wird um Mitteilung gebeten.~~

Leutnant und Hilfsoffizier

Reservelazarett Bad Wörishofen

Teillazarett Kneipplanum

Formblatt 6 b zu H.Dv. 21 II. Teil

27.3.45

....

(Lazarett)
(Datum)

An

Jg.Ers.Batl.49

(Feldtruppenteil oder Ersatztruppenteil)

Der   Gefr. Heinz Gebhardt

(Dienstgrad, Vorname, Zuname)

1.Kp.Batl.IV Kampfgr.Mohr

(letzter Feldtruppenteil, nicht Feldpost-Nr.)

ist am   21.3.45   durch den Chefarzt des   Reserve-   Lazarett

Bad Wörishofen   mit dem Verwundetenabzeichen in — Schwarz —

Silber — Gold — beliehen worden, — und zwar ohne Rücksicht auf die Zahl

der Verwundungen — *). Er ist nach wehrmachtärztlichem Urteil Schwerst-

beschädigter. Es besteht Versehrtenstufe **) *) .... Seine dauernde

Wehrdienstunfähigkeit — steht fest — ist — nicht — wahrscheinlich — läßt

sich noch nicht beurteilen.

Die sanitätsdienstlichen Voraussetzungen zur Verleihung des E.K. 2 für

Schwerverwundete liegen vor. Ein diesbezüglicher Vorschlag ist von hier aus

am .... bei ....

gemacht worden *).

Die sanitätsdienstlichen Voraussetzungen zur Beförderung zum nächst-

höheren Dienstgrad gemäß H.Dv. 29 a Ziffer 37 Abs. 4 liegen vor *).

....

(Unterschrift)

Leitender Arzt u. Stabsarzt

....

(Dienstgrad und Dienststellung)

*) Nichtzutreffendes ist zu streichen.
**) Nur ausfüllen, wenn Versehrtenstufe III oder IV (siehe Rückseite) besteht.

159 W. Druckerei VII, München 11. 44

Form 6 b

BESITZZEUGNIS

DEM

Gefr. Heinz Gebhardt
(NAME, DIENSTGRAD)

1.Kp.Batl.IV Regt. Mohr
(TRUPPENTEIL, DIENSTSTELLE)

IST AUF GRUND

SEINER AM ⎯⎯ 26. 2. 1945 ⎯⎯ ERLITTENEN

3 MALIGEN VERWUNDUNG – BESCHÄDIGUNG

DAS

VERWUNDETENABZEICHEN

IN Silber

VERLIEHEN WORDEN.

Bad=Wörishofen, DEN 21. 3. 194 5

Dr. P. L. Baumgarten.
(UNTERSCHRIFT)

Oberfeldarzt und Chefarzt
Res. Lazarett Bad=Wörishofen
(DIENSTGRAD UND DIENSTSTELLE)

**Possession certificate for the Wound Badge in Silver
for a knee-joint shot sustained in the fortress of Breslau.**

26.2-45

Gefr. Heinz Gebhardt.

Kniegelenkschuss re. Punktion ergibt reines Blut
Wundausschneidung Gelenkkapsel nicht eröffnet. Gips-
verband.
    T.A.T. noch nicht erhalten.========== (im August 1944 SeeuTAT.
                                              erhalten)

8.III. 3000 A.E. T.A.T. intramusk. gegeben.
                        Fr. bei Rudlec.

Wolfgang Kolbe. His wound by an artillery shell cost him his right leg. As a severely wounded soldier, he was promoted to *Unteroffizier* and awarded the Silver Wound Badge and the Iron Cross II. Class.

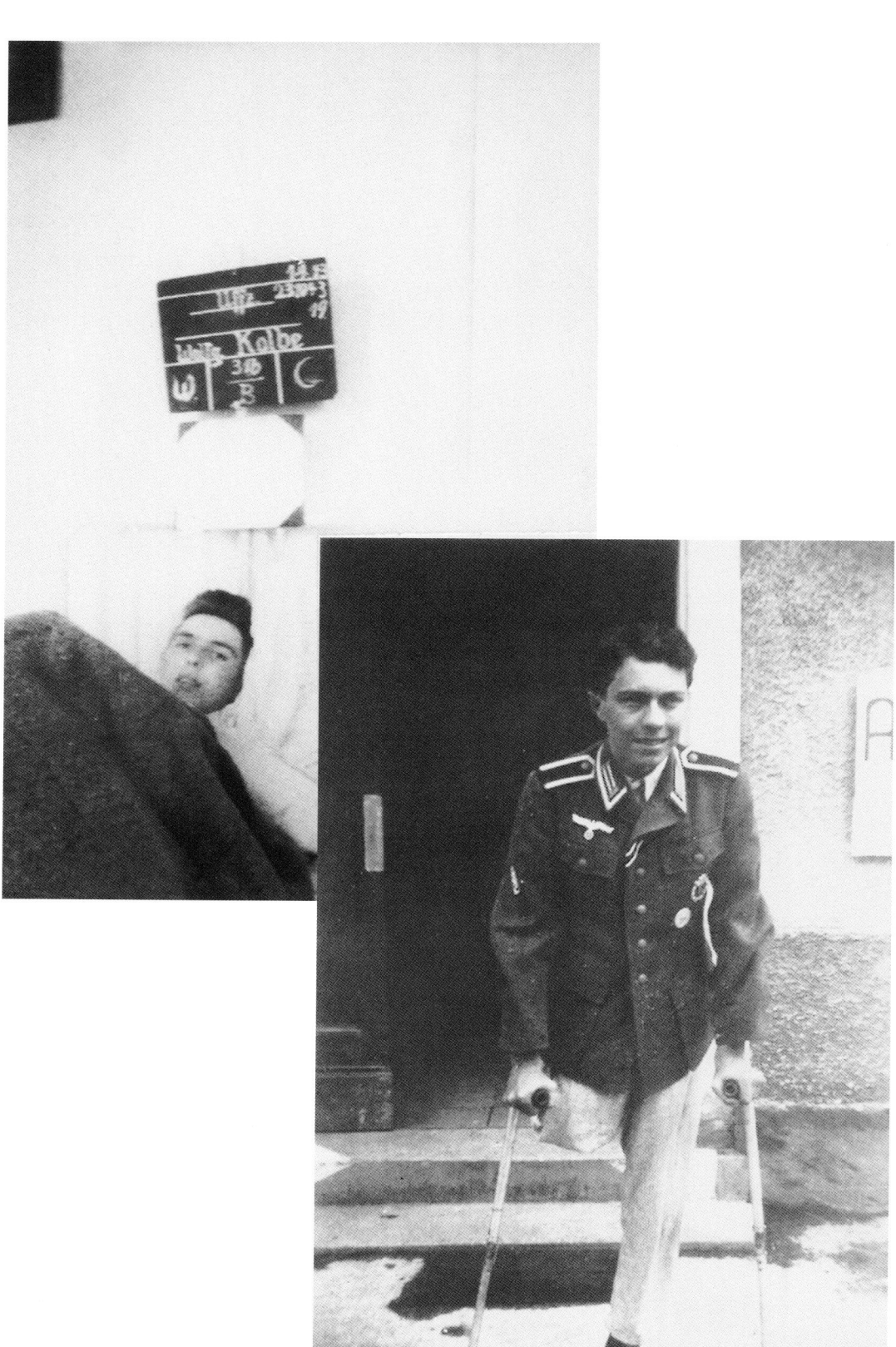

Besitzeugnis

der

Ehefrau

Johanna Schneidereit

ist auf Grund

ihrer am   28. Mai 1944   erlittenen

ein-maligen Verwundung oder Beschädigung

das

Verwundetenabzeichen

in   S c h w a r z

verliehen worden

Königsberg (Pr), den 8.September   194 4

Der Kommandierende General
und Befehlshaber im Luftgau I

General der Flieger

B.L. 11/44/4

Possession certificate for the Wound Badge in Black for
a woman civilian wounded in an Allied air raid.

FRAU ANNA NEUKIRCHEN!

ZU DER VERLEIHUNG DES

Verwundeten-
abzeichen

IN GOLD

DAS IHNEN FÜR DIE AM
1. AUGUST 1942
DURCH TERRORANGRIFF ERLITTENE
VERWUNDUNG ÜBERREICHT WIRD,
BEGLÜCKWÜNSCHT SIE UND DANKT
FÜR DIE TAPFERE HALTUNG DIE

NSDAP.

ORTSGRUPPE SÖMMERDA-FICHTE

Document of the Nazi Party Soemmerda-Fichte local group for awarding the
Wound Badge in Gold to a woman who was wounded during an Allied air raid.

BIBLIOGRAPHY

Reich Law Sheet, Part I
No.160 of September 3, 1939, p.1577

Army Regulation Sheet, Part A
Of September 8, 1939, p.77 f. No.83
Of October 11, 1939, p.110 No.113

General Army Announcements
Of April 7, 1943, p.211 No.302 and 305
Of January 24, 1944, p.24 No.46 ff.

Uniform Market of September 15, 1937, p.286.

Absolon, Richard, "Wehrgesetz und Wehrdienst 1935-1945". *Das Personalwesen in der Wehrmacht*, Boppard, 1960.

Hessenthal, Horst von, "Das Verwundetenabzeichen, Zu seiner Stiftung vor 60 Jahren", in *Deutsches Soldatenjahrbuch* 1978, p.233, Munich, 1978.

Michaelis, Rolf, *Die Geschichte der Deutschen Verwundetenabzeichen*, Erlangen 1992.

Michaelis, Rolf, *Die Deutschen Verwundetenabzeichen*, Erlangen, 1995.

OTHER BOOKS BY ROLF MICHAELIS

SS-Heimwehr Danzig in Poland 1939

SS-Fallschirmjäger-Bataillon 500/600

The 10th SS-Panzer-Division "Frundsberg"

The 11th SS-Freiwilligen-Panzer-Grenadier-Division "Nordland"

The 32nd SS-Freiwilligen-Grenadier-Division: "30.Januar"

Combat Operations of the German Ordnungspolizei,
1939-1945: Polizei-Bataillone • SS-Polizei-Regimenter

Cavalry Divisions of the Waffen-SS

Panzergrenadier Divisions of the Waffen-SS

The Kaminski Brigade

Belgians in the Waffen-SS

The German Sniper Badge 1944-1945

The German Tank Destruction Badge in World War II